JESUS, the Morning Star!

"JESUS in 100 Ways" Series

Papa & Mama Goose

JESUS, The Morning Star!
"JESUS in 100 Ways" Series

Papa & Mama Goose

Copyright © 2020
Enchanted Rose Publishing
P.O. Box 991
Hempstead, TX 77445

Published by Enchanted Rose Publishing
Layout by Cynthia D. Johnson @
www.diverseskillscenter.com

Written by Papa & Mama Goose

Printed in the United States of America
ISBN-13: 978-1-947799-70-7

When I go to school, I see my friend Mario.

Mario got loads of brand-new sneakers and jackets for back to school.

My friends seem to have the best clothes compared to mine.

Then, I think to myself...I may not have much, but I have JESUS.

Mandy talks about the wonderful vacations her family took during the summer.

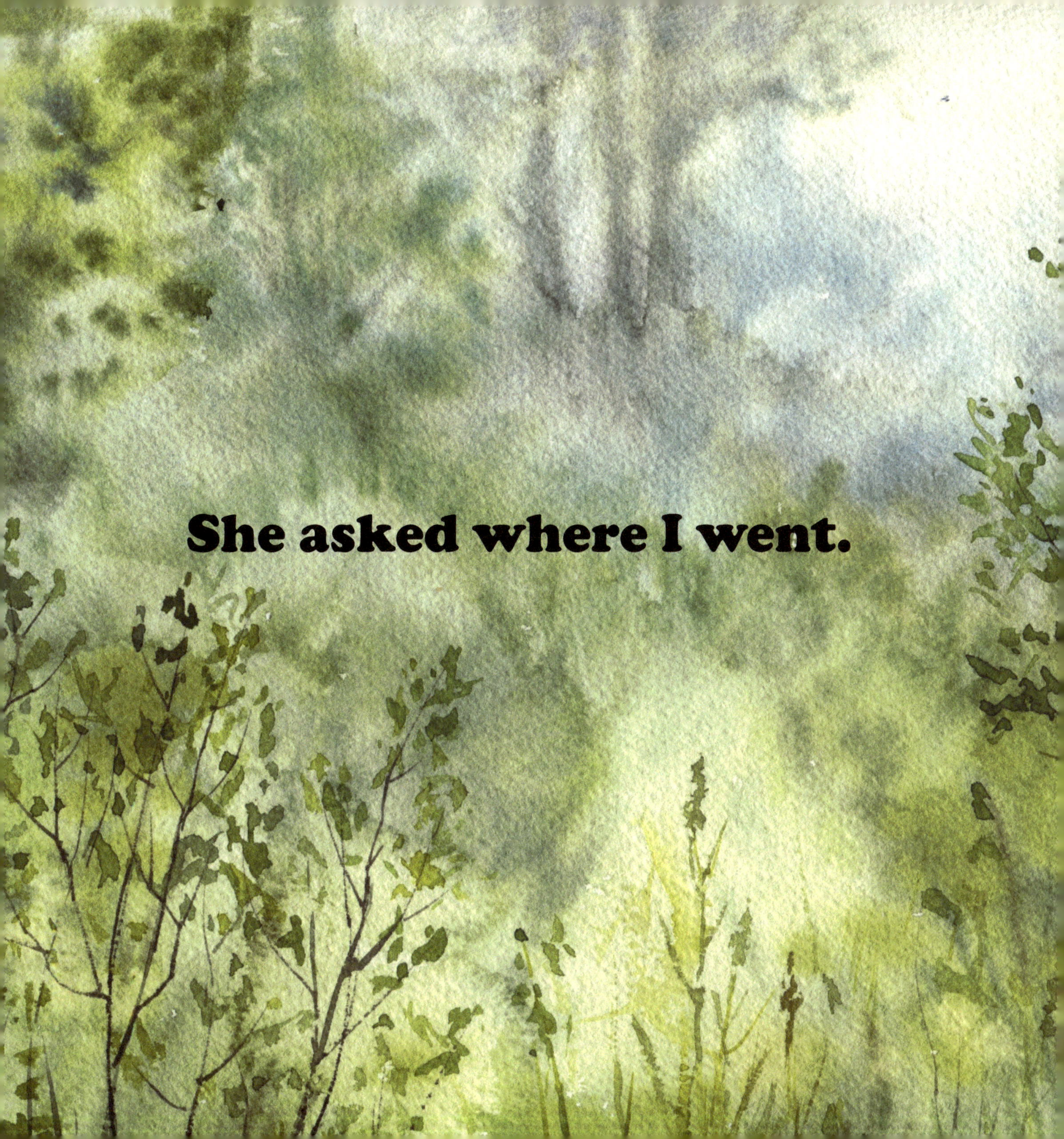

She asked where I went.

I said, "You wouldn't believe me if I told you!"

When I face problems or something happens in life that I don't understand, I visit my Bible.

It takes me through the mind of GOD, a place like no other.

When I feel lost and can't seem to find my way, I look to JESUS, my bright and morning Star.

When JESUS is around, the darkness flees.

One candle can illuminate even the darkest of rooms.

When the night is long, and I cannot find my peace, I then see my Morning Star, JESUS.

JESUS'S brightness always comes in the darkest hours.

JESUS can dispel any sorrow I may face in the past, present, and future.

Weeping may endure for a night and temporarily pull my spirit down, but my Joy will rise before the dawn.

My soul will wait.

My soul will wait on JESUS.

When I see the Morning Star on the horizon, I know that my blues will fly away.

I can lean on my Morning Star.

I can depend on Him.

JESUS is my Joy!

JESUS is my bright and

Morning Star...

Scripture Reference

2 Peter 1:18-21;

Revelation 22:12-16

JESUS, The Morning Star!

"JESUS in 100 Ways" Series

Written by Papa & Mama Goose

Copyright 2020

by

Mama Goose Books

Hempstead, Texas

Papa & Mama Goose Media

Through the power of their faith and instructions from GOD's HOLY SPIRIT, these humble servants of CHRIST take us back to our beginning...The Bible. Although Papa and Mama Goose have written a plethora of books, none can hold a candle to how the WORD of GOD has guided their lives. Realizing that life on Earth is temporal, Papa and Mama Goose wanted to write Books about the Bible that would provide a Biblical Foundation for young children. The goal of the books is to teach youngsters to know and fall deeply in Love with GOD.

It was during their years in college that Papa and Mama Goose found CHRIST. They were taught the Gospel and baptized into the Prairie View CHURCH of CHRIST at Prairie View A & M University in Prairie View, Texas. Papa and Mama Goose enjoy sharing the same spiritual birthday. Currently, the dynamic duo are faithful members of the Fifth Ward CHURCH of CHRIST in Houston, Texas.

Follow Me On...

 Facebook

www.facebook.com/gomamagoose

 Twitter

@GoMamaGoose

 Instagram

MamaGoose Paris

gomamagoose@gmail.com